D1404000

JOSEPH MIDTHUN   SAMUEL HITI

FRACTIONS

Buzz

WORLD
BOOK

www.worldbook.com

World Book, Inc.
180 North LaSalle Street
Suite 900
Chicago, Illinois 60601
USA

For information about other World Book publications,
visit our website at www.worldbook.com
or call 1-800-WORLDBK (967-5325).
For information about sales to schools and libraries,
call 1-800-975-3250 (United States),
or 1-800-837-5365 (Canada).

Building Blocks of Mathematics:
  Fractions
ISBN: 978-0-7166-7894-6 (trade, hc.)
ISBN: 978-0-7166-1475-3 (pbk.)
ISBN: 978-0-7166-1873-7 (e-book, EPUB3)
ISBN: 978-0-7166-2443-1 (e-book, PDF)

Acknowledgments:
Created by Samuel Hiti and Joseph Midthun
Art by Samuel Hiti
Text by Joseph Midthun
Special thanks to Anita Wager,
Hala Ghousseini, and Syril McNally

TABLE OF CONTENTS

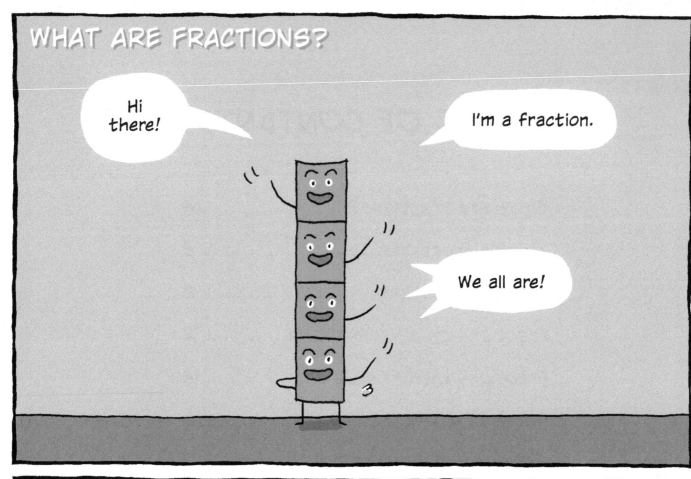

The number on top is called the numerator.

It tells you how many equal parts we are counting.

The bottom number is called the denominator.

It tells you how many equal parts the whole is divided into.

When we count one-third of the rectangle...

...we are counting 1 of the 3 equal parts.

1, 2, 3!

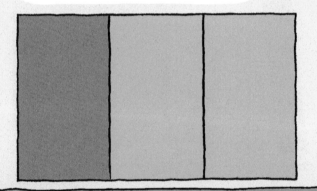

Writing fractions like this is okay, too...

...as long as the numerator and denominator are clearly separated by a line!

There are countless numbers of fractions!

Let's just focus on a few common ones.

A whole square!

$\frac{1}{2}$ is called a half.

Buzz

It represents 1 of 2 equal parts.

Buzz

Oh!

A whole circle!

Buzz

Take that!

Buzz

Buzz

Buzz

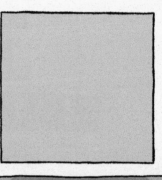

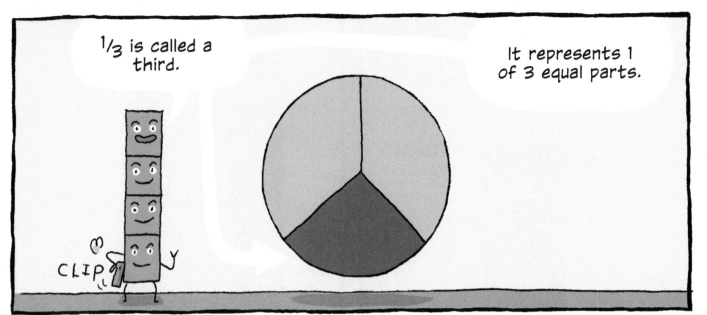

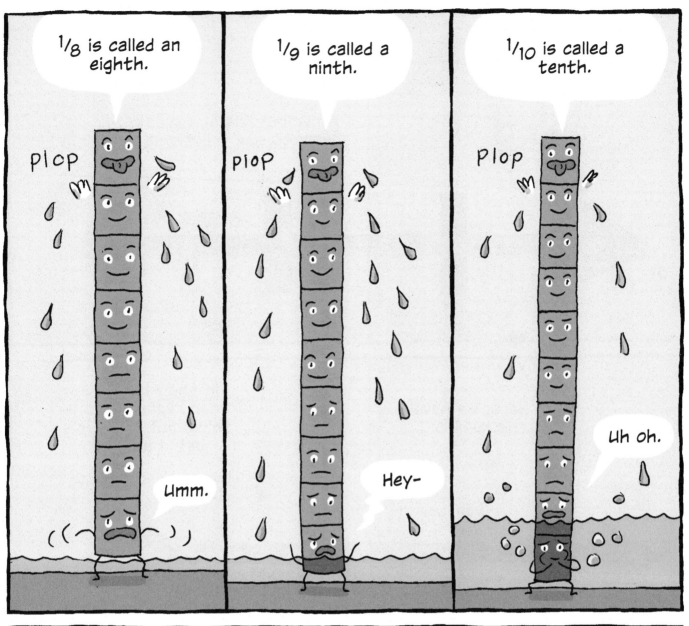

FRACTIONS ON A NUMBER LINE

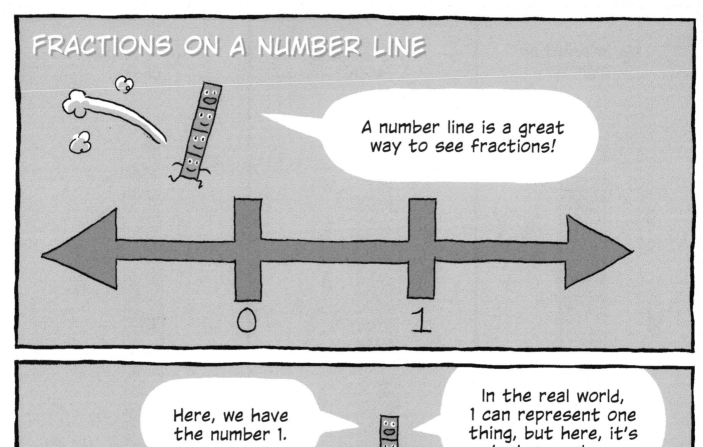

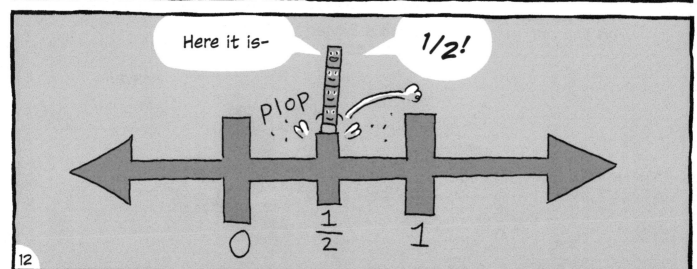

13

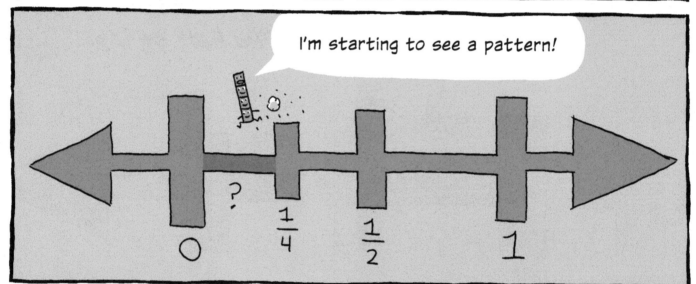

15

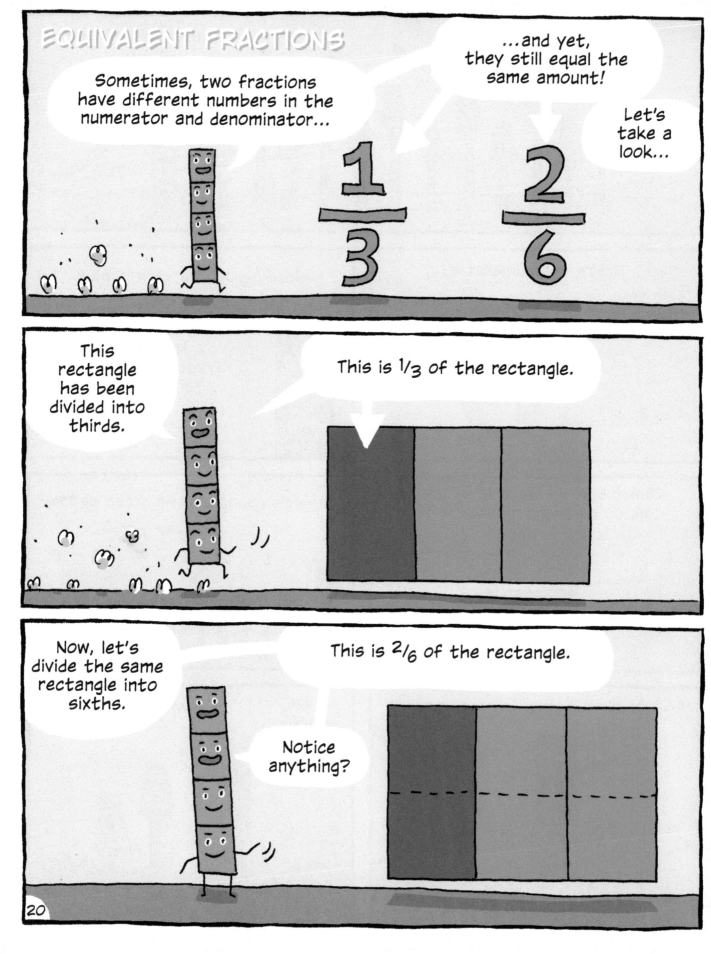

The same amount of area is shaded.

So, 1/3 and 2/6 are equal!

They are *equivalent fractions!*

Let's look at another example.

This is 1/2 of a circle.

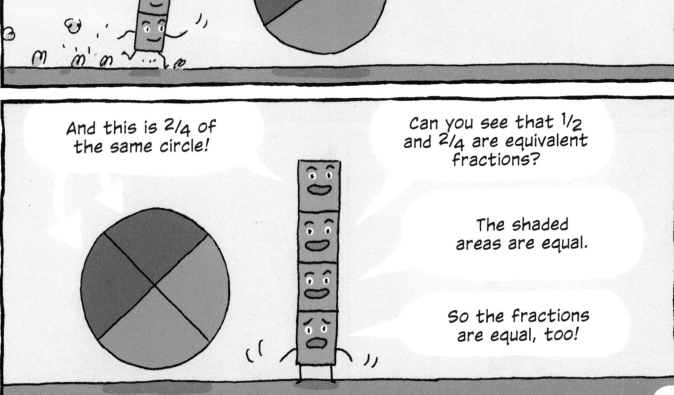

And this is 2/4 of the same circle!

Can you see that 1/2 and 2/4 are equivalent fractions?

The shaded areas are equal.

So the fractions are equal, too!

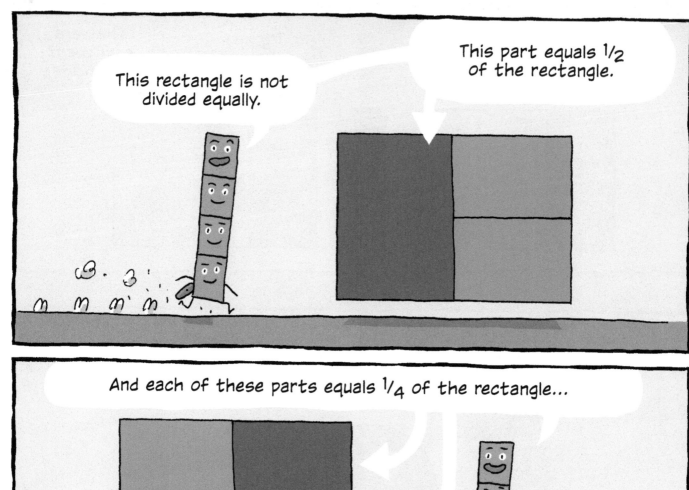

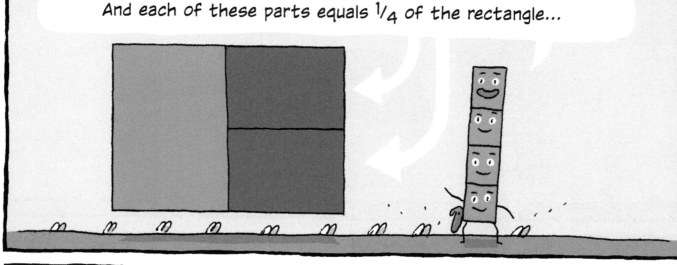

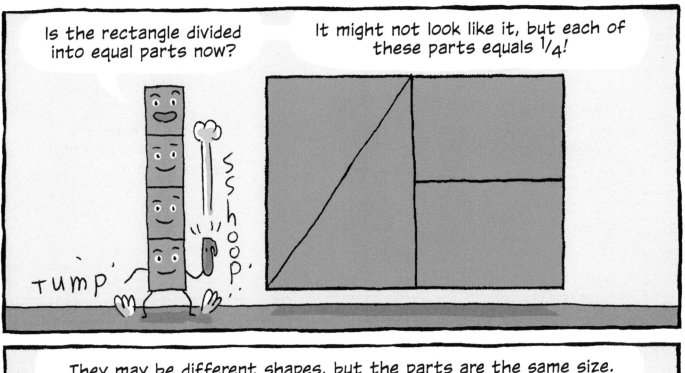

What if we want to compare fractions?

It's easy to compare fractions with matching denominators...

For instance, which is the larger fraction:

$$\frac{3}{10}$$

$$\frac{9}{10}$$

If you have 3 equal parts of 10, it would look like this...

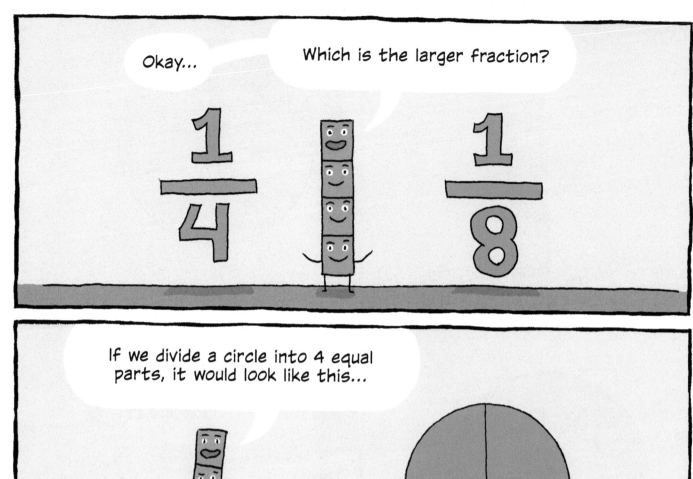

Okay...

Which is the larger fraction?

If we divide a circle into 4 equal parts, it would look like this...

If we divide the same object into 8 equal parts, it would look like this...

FRACTIONS ALL AROUND

If you look closely, you'll find that fractions are all around you.

In fact, even you represent a fraction!

You're one part of the entire population of the world!

Earth is a fraction of the solar system.

The solar system is a fraction of the galaxy.

The galaxy is a fraction of the universe.

We are how you can describe all of these things.

So remember, if you ever need to describe an amount that is part of a whole...

...or, even a whole amount...

...use us!

We're Fractions!

29

FRACTION FACTS

The diagrams on this page can help you see several common fractions. Remember, fractions come from breaking a whole into equal parts.

FRACTIONS

	1
	$\frac{1}{2}$
	$\frac{1}{3}$
	$\frac{1}{4}$
	$\frac{1}{5}$
	$\frac{1}{6}$
	$\frac{1}{7}$
	$\frac{1}{8}$
	$\frac{1}{9}$
	$\frac{1}{10}$

FRACTION NAMES

Whole

Halves

Thirds

Fourths

Fifths

Sixths

Sevenths

Eighths

Ninths

Tenths

FIND OUT MORE

BOOKS

Eat Your Math Homework:
Recipes for Hungry Minds
    by Ann McCallum
    and Leeza Hernandez
    (Charlesbridge, 2011)

Fabulous Fractions: Games and
Activities That Make Math Easy
and Fun
    by Lynette Long
    (Wiley, 2001)

Fractions, Decimals, and Percents
    by David A. Adler
    and Edward Miller
    (Holiday House, 2010)

Fractions and Decimals Made Easy
    by Rebecca Wingard-Nelson
    (Enslow Publishers, 2005)

A Fraction's Goal: Parts of a Whole
    by Brian P. Cleary
    and Brian Gable
    (Millbrook Press, 2011)

If You Were a Fraction
    by Trisha Speed Shaskan
    and Francesca Carabelli
    (Picture Window Books, 2009)

Riddle-iculous Math
    by Joan Holub
    and Regan Dunnick
    (A. Whitman, 2003)

What's a Fraction?
    by Nancy Kelly Allen
    (Rourke Publishing, 2012)

WEBSITES

A+ Click
    http://www.aplusclick.com/
    arithmetic.htm
    Test all your different kinds of math
    skills with the games and practice
    activities here.

Cool Math 4 Kids: Fractions
    http://www.coolmath4kids.com/
    fractions
    Try out the lessons and practice games
    at this educational website.

Funschool: Number Games
    http://funschool.kaboose.com/
    formula-fusion/number-fun
    With games like Action Fraction, this
    site makes learning math a blast.

Math Is Fun: Fractions
    http://www.mathsisfun.com/
    fractions-menu.html
    This site has options for learning about
    fractions at many difficulty levels.

Melvin's Make-a-Match Game
    http://pbskids.org/cyberchase/
    math-games/melvins-make-match
    Help Melvin sort out his laboratory with
    your fraction skills!

PrimaryGames: Pizza Party
    http://www.primarygames.com/
    fractions/start.htm
    Use your fraction knowledge to
    figure out how much pizza is left
    for the party.

NOTE TO EDUCATORS

This volume supports a conceptual understanding of fractions. With the Fractions character as their guide, children are introduced to different representations of fractions, including set, area, and measurement models. Below is an index of concepts that appear in this volume. For more information about how to teach fractions in the classroom, see the list of Educator Resources at the bottom of this page.

Index of Strategies

Educator Resources

Children's Mathematics: Cognitively Guided Instruction
by Thomas Carpenter, Elizabeth Fennema, Megan L. Franke, Linda Levi, and Susan B. Empson (Heinemann, 1999)

Elementary and Middle School Mathematics: Teaching Developmentally
by John A. Van de Walle, Karen S. Karp, and Jennifer M. Bay-Williams (Harcourt, 2013)

Knowing and Teaching Elementary Mathematics: Teachers' Understanding of Fundamental Mathematics in China and the United States
by Liping Ma (Routledge, 2010)

Young Mathematicians at Work:
Constructing Fractions, Decimals, and Percents
by Catherine Twomey Fosnot and Maarten Dolk (Heinemann, 2011)

CPSIA information can be obtained
at www.ICGtesting.com
Printed in the USA
LVOW06*1441070217

523491LV00020B/373/P